I0488280

Breaking the Bank with Amazon Kindle - How to Create a Kindle Bestseller in 6 Simple Steps

By Eugene Walker

SMASHWORDS EDITION

PUBLISHED BY:
TKM MASON GROUP,LLC ON SMASHWORDS

DISCLAIMER

Table of Contents

Chapter 1 - Introduction
Chapter 2 - The Multi-Billion Dollar Kindle Opportunity
Chapter 3 - Why Kindle Publishing is one of The Best Online Businesses Today!
Chapter 4 - Let's Count the Money and Do the Math Here!
Chapter 5 - Real Case Studies on Kindle
Chapter 6 - How to Create a Kindle Bestseller in 6 Simple Steps
Chapter 7 - Your Kindle Publishing Opportunity
Chapter 8 - How to Use Public Domain Products as a Template for Creating Your Books
Chapter 9 - The Top Websites Where You Can Find Ideas on Which E-books Sell Best
Chapter 10 - More Tips on Promoting Your E-book and getting it Out to The World
Chapter 11 - Other Types of Marketing
Chapter 12 - 59 Places to Submit Your Free KDP Promotion for Your Kindle eBook
Chapter 13 - ACCESS TO BONUS STEP-BY-STEP VIDEO TUTORIALS

Chapter 1 - Introduction

Welcome to "How to Create a Kindle Bestseller in 6 Simple Steps". Here is where you will discover how to leverage Amazon's 400 million customers to make a full time income while working part time publishing Kindle books. You will also learn to position yourself as an expert in your field if you apply the stuff outlined in this book and take action.

Here are some of the things we are going to cover in this short book. The book is going to be divided up into 5 main parts and in part 1, I want to go and give you an overview of the multi-billion dollar kindle opportunity. Now you might know some of this stuff already but it is really quite impressive stuff and worth going over again. In part 2,

How to Create a Kindle Bestseller in 6 Simple Steps I will give you a couple of case studies on how 2 books got to #1 and #2 bestseller status respectively by following this exact system outlined in this book.

In part 3, I am going to show you the 6 step system to creating a bestseller. So I will take you through the whole process, (simplified step by step) so you can apply it to your own books in the future. In part 4, I am going to talk about your Kindle publishing opportunity. I will take you through that opportunity and what is on the course and how you can get involved if you want to take this a step further. Then in part 5, I will answer many common questions people may have about Kindle publishing, so that is going to be the format of this book.

Chapter 2 - The Multi-Billion Dollar Kindle Opportunity

So let's kick it straight off with part 1 which is the multi-billion dollar Kindle opportunity. Going back to 2010, e-book sales were worth $1.2 billion which is pretty good, but in just 2 years by 2012 that number had gone up to 4.3 billion. So it had increased and gone up over 300%. Here is the thing, by 2016 it is predicted to go up to 10.9 billion and growing and this is just in (North America) alone. There is the whole rest of the world available to be reached through Kindle. So if you've got a book that is selling well in North America for example, you can translate it into other languages really cheaply and put it in front of the whole world and not only that 10.9 billion market in North America.

So I wanted to tell you that first because Kindle wasn't launched until 2007 and had a lot of catching up to do, but within a couple of years, sales began to shoot upwards dramatically! By April of 2011, Amazon had sold more Kindle books than paperback and hardback (combined). Now that just gives you an idea on how quickly Amazon

Kindle is growing and what an amazing opportunity this is to get a pie of that billion dollar pie. It has now become an expectation that Amazon will sell twice as many Kindle books as physical books. This is why Kindle publishing is one of the best online businesses today.

Chapter 3 - Why Kindle Publishing is one of The Best Online Businesses Today!

Here are a few reasons why it might certainly be one of the best online businesses today. First of all it costs nothing to get started; publishing on KDP is completely free. Secondly there is zero overhead because everything you put into Amazon is managed for free through Amazon. You make up to 70% profit on sales (which is huge). A typical author going through a traditional publisher (especially a first time author) would tend to around 10% royalties and that is (maybe). Compared to the 70% you get on Kindle, this is a 700% increase on what you would get through a traditional publisher.

In fact some traditional authors that have already succeeded traditionally are actually switching away from their publishers and onto Kindle because the royalty module is better. Another big thing is that Amazon takes care of the back end for you so you don't have to process anything. You don't have to ship anything out. You don't have to take care of customer service. If somebody wants a refund it is taken care of. You don't have to worry about anything except getting your book published.

Here is another one and this is huge, Amazon markets your book for you and that is kind of what this book is about, how to leverage Amazon and get them to market your book for you. Amazon can do more to market your books than anyone else ever could because they are the biggest book store in the world. Another great thing about Amazon is you can be published and selling within less than 24 hours, now obviously that is 24 hours after you manuscript is ready to go. Another great thing with Kindle it doesn't have to be a 200 page book. A 10 or 20 thousand word small book or short story on Kindle works perfectly well as long as the content is good. It can be up and selling in 24 hours!

Chapter 4 - Let's Count the Money and Do the Math Here!

I want to give you a simple math example to show you what can be achieved on Kindle, and again I am being quite conservative about the numbers here. Let's take for example you only sold 10 copies a day of a $4.99 book. Now I say $4.99 because that is a sweet spot for a Kindle book. People expect to pay a little bit less than they would for a physical copy, so $4.99 at 70% royalties and 10 copies a day will give you $35 a day. Now if you add that up at the end of the month that is over $1,000 a month.

Now 10 copies a day is a very achievable number, and although it is not knocking it out of the park, it is very achievable with the things I am going to teach you. So if you can do 10 copies a day that is $1,000 a month. Ok, so what if we scale that up? What if we go from 1 book to 5 books? Now were onto $5239 per month which gives you $62,874 a year! So you get the idea! It is like anything else, you have to put some work into producing those books and there are ways of outsourcing books as well.

Outsourcing can allow you to build up a portfolio a lot quicker and you can do that reasonably cheaply as well. So you get the idea on how you can start to build up a pretty good royalty stream pretty quickly, and just gradually build on that until you can replace your full time income with Kindle books.

Ok, so that was just some numbers to give you an idea on what you can do on Kindle, now here is something else. Imagine if you're an expert, coach, speaker, have an existing business, or you have an information product you want to sell. If you have a service or product business, having an e-book out there is a way to build massive credibility for you and your business. It also establishes you as an expert in your space and this is a bonus! This is in addition to any royalties you would be getting.

So it can be really powerful positioning for you if you want to position yourself as an expert and maybe build a back end around your books. To tie in very well with that is you can build an email list of buyers, so you can have a call to action in your book that allows people to subscribe to a mailing list where you can start to build a relationship with those people and then when you have built a relationship with them you get to sell to them products or services that meet their needs. So it is a really powerful way of building a business.

Chapter 5 - Real Case Studies on Kindle

So let's get into part 2 now, which is those two case studies that I mentioned to you earlier because it demonstrates the results you can get if you try these things.

Here is case study #1.

Steve was a corporate lawyer; he used to work in the city of London as a corporate lawyer and spent several years doing it even though his heart wasn't really in it. So in 2009 he set up an online real estate company and as part of that process began to learn about online marketing. He had spent a lot of money learning about online marketing and gradually built an online business in 2012 that sold over $200,000 of services online.

But as time went on he ended up losing a lot of money. The reason was because the business had really high overheads, and was very labour intensive. Steve had hired 3 extra full time workers so there was a lot of staffing overheads and telephone operatives as well.

Steve had surveyors that used to go out to properties for him and all that had to be paid for. So it cost about $236,000 to run the business which meant he lost about $36,000 which is about $3000 a month. So basically Steve was in the enviable position of working very hard to go slowly broke which is not good business at all. So finally Steve closed shop and wound that business up, because it made no sense to be losing $3000 a month and working really hard to do that.

Meanwhile Steve had written 4 books by that point, and his first book was a thriller that he had written in 1998. Steve sent manuscripts out to lots of agents and couldn't get an agent. Now as you may know, if you can't get an agent to represent you, it is near on impossible to get a publisher to look at your manuscript. So having gone so far with it, Steve gave up and shelved the project for a few months.

Steve came back a few years later in 2004 and wrote a book about diet and weight loss and again it was the same situation, he couldn't get an agent even though the feedback was actually very positive. People would tell him "Well, it is a good book…but the market is really saturated right now" "It is going to need some kind of celebrity angle or some kind of celebrity endorsement if we are going to represent this."

So again it got so far but didn't get off the ground, and that was the old school pre-Kindle world. Back then you had to rely on the gatekeeper i.e. the agent as to whether you had the chance of getting published or not.

So roll on to mid-2012 this is when Steve had discovered Kindle publishing or Kindle Direct Publishing (KDP). Having found out about

Kindle publishing and how it all works, he decided in October 2012 to write a book about real estate, and to promote and re-position himself and his online business. He had a lot of content on his website that he had written so he was able to repurpose a lot of that and put a book together. Once he finished with that he had figured out how to market it. Please note: You can have the best book in the world but if you don't know how to market it, it is not going to sell very well.

So to make a long story short, in December 2012 and January 2013 his book went on to become a 3 time #1 best seller on Amazon (in the paid category). In that very first month in January it made $1,984 and that was just in the first month in a niche category. So compare that to the previous business which was losing up to $3000 a month. So now Steve was banking $2,000 a month in profit. So this is one of the reasons Kindle publishing is one of the great modules in our time!

Here is case study #2.

Here is a second example. Steve wrote another book on dieting back in 2004 and published it at the end of March. During the free give away (that is one of the things we will talk about that is in one of the 6 steps by the way if you are already familiar with the KDP select free give away) it got 15,700 downloads in the first 5 days. So that is a lot of downloads for a nonfiction book and the book was focused purely on the Kindle marketing.

If you were in health and fitness and you were trying to build a list of people and you had a link at the beginning of the book to get people to opt into your list, let's say you had a 20% conversion rate on that list, that would be over 3,000 people opting into your list in just 5 days. So it would be a fantastic way and a super, super quick way of launching a brand new business because you can do pretty well with

3000 subscribers especially if they like your stuff and you build a relationship with them.

It hit number 37 overall on Kindle, and while it was free it was also a number one bestseller in four categories. Ok so that was while it was FREE. Now this is what happened when it switched to paid. Now that it had a lot of momentum from all those free downloads and a lot of advertising of the book across Amazon, It was able to hit number 2 in weight loss which is a super competitive category.

Weight loss is a huge category in fact. But at the same time it hit number 2 in the weight loss category, the book also hit number 247 on ALL OF KINDLE! Now this is for PAID BOOKS and just to put that into perspective there are (over 2 million) books on Kindle. So out of over 2 million books Steve's book was ranked number 247 out of all of them. The book ended up bringing in up to 423 sales a day.

Here is the thing. The book was kind of a feedback loop which was the goal in the first place. Once the book started hitting a tipping point; Amazon start doing the work from then on. So the more sales you get the more visibility you get and the more visibility you get the more sales you get and so on and so on. So it feeds on itself and that is where we are trying to get your books to and that is what this 6 step system is about.

Chapter 6 - How to Create a Kindle Bestseller in 6 Simple Steps

That is 2 case studies there showing you the possibilities of using the system which leads us very neatly into part 3 which is, "How to Create a Kindle Bestseller in 6 Simple Steps".

Just a quick recap over what this 6 steps is about, Amazon is the world's biggest buyer search engine. We know Google is the number one search engine but the number one buyer search engine is Amazon. Amazon is also the world's biggest book shop. They sold over 400 million Kindle books in 2012 and conservatively they are expected to be 40% higher than that in the future, if not more.

So with the Kindle app there is like 5 billion devices in the world that are capable of downloading Kindle books with that app. It is the world's most trusted online retailer. They have 400 million plus credit cards on file which allows one click purchasing which is fantastic for us as it makes Kindle books into the ultimate impulse purchase which is great for us to market. So the reason I am giving you that little bit of background there is we want to leverage this incredible power of Amazon and Kindle and get Amazon to do the heavy lifting for us, we want to be focused on building our business writing our books, and creating our content.

If we choose to outsource your books, you don't have to worry about managing that process and constantly coming back and marketing. This is all about setting your books up so Amazon will do that for you. But to achieve that we have to get to that tipping point that I talked about where Amazon starts promoting it for you and putting your book in front of that super highly charged audience. We have seen an example of that with the 2 case studies earlier. The result is going to be organic and long term sales. Ok so let's get straight into those 6 steps to make that happen.

Step #1 Create an Attention Grabbing Title.

The title has 2 roles. Firstly it is to grab the attention of your prospect (which is absolutely paramount) and the second is to help your book rank in both Amazon search and Google search. Amazon is obviously crucial because that is where your buyers are but you have a chance to rank on Google as well, particularly if you are targeting certain keywords (which we will talk about in a moment).

The reason this can work really well for you on Google is that Amazon is such a high authority website that Amazon pages often rank quite highly, particularly if people are searching for something and they put the word books at the end of it. You virtually see that the top couple of pages will have Amazon links. So you can leverage the power of Amazon to get yourself up the Google rankings in a way you couldn't do if you were doing this on your own website.

What we are going to do ideally with our title and our subtitle is a mixture of short, medium and long-tail keywords. It is very important that the title and the subtitle work well together. (I will come back to how these relate to one another in a second) but first I want to take you through the search rankings first. We will go through Amazon and Google search and how to look up keywords for those and once we have done that we will go through the grabbing attention part.

So setting out the key words for your title is a two stage process, first of all we are going to go to the Google keyword tool and use that to create a short list and then secondly we are going to filter that short list through Amazon's Kindle store search. **Please note:** (Google's keyword tool has now been changed to keyword planner…you will have to open up a Google AdWords account to get this feature now)

Let's do a quick demonstration. Let's say we wanted to write a book on "The Paleo Diet" (which by the way is very popular on Amazon). What we can do is go to our Google keyword planner, type in the keyword "Paleo Diet" and a list of good ideas should pop up and show you the amount of traffic each keyword is getting. Now in terms of the number of people looking for those keywords, 10,000 searches a month is ideal.

Now you might be in one of those situations where one of the keyword phrases has less than 10,000 searches but is very similar to what you're looking for. But if there is less than 10,000 people a month searching, then it is probably not worth going after since it is just too niche and you are not going to make the sales there.

So once you have your short list from Google; you want to go from there into Amazon and do a search in Amazon. First thing you want to do is make sure you are searching within the Kindle store because you want to look at what people are buying. If you type in Paleo diets without hitting ENTER on your computer (a drop box of more search terms will appear underneath). Now you can start cross checking your short list from Google against what people are actually looking for on Kindle itself. Basically Amazon will tell you what people are looking for specifically (down in the drop box).

That is the two stage process for creating a short list using the Google keyword planner which is free and then the Amazon Kindle store search which is also free. You can use both of these tools to filter out and create a really good list of ideas of you can put in your title and subtitle. This method is good for ranking high on Amazon and Google together.

Now having done that let's go onto the attention grabbing bit, so what I want you to think about when you're crafting your headlines is keep thinking… (Newspaper Headlines). When you pick up a newspaper you tend to not read the whole thing…you first stop…and if a headline takes your attention you read the article underneath it. It also works the other way round, if the headline doesn't grab your attention you move on and ignore the article completely.

It is exactly the same with your books. The title has a number of roles to perform. First and foremost it has to grab attention. It shouldn't be too long and difficult but easy to read. A little alliteration is also good because it makes it memorable and easy to understand. Your book should also speak to your target market and let them know that the book is for them. It does no good to grab the attention of the wrong people, so it has got to speak to your target market and at least have something in there that says the book is relevant to them.

Ideally you want your title to be either exciting or controversial. You can also try making a big promise. That promise could be that you are going to save them some kind of pain, or there is going to be some kind of pleasure. Maybe you are going to solve a problem for them, or if it is a fiction book you are promising entertainment and escapism. Now here is the thing and this is so important... without a good title you get no click on your thumbnail on Amazon and no sale. So it doesn't matter how good the book is, if you don't get the click you have lost the sale. Because what will happen is they will click on somebody else's book with a more interesting title, read there description and then end up buying that book and not yours.

Adding Your Subtitle

Ok so now let's talk about adding your subtitle. So I have talked about how the subtitle can work with the title and one of the things you can do with your subtitle is make it significantly longer than the title. The title should be short and attention grabbing but the subtitle can be longer. So the title should hook them in and if they like the title and they are interested enough to go to the next step then they will read your subtitle. The subtitle is where you can insert some of your keywords.

Here is a great tip. If you have got a great title which grabs attention and tells people what the book is about, don't sacrifice a great title in the expense of keywords. A great title is more important than the keywords. Something else I should mention as well before I go on through the rest of these steps is most fictional authors don't use a subtitle but it is a really good marketing tip to use a subtitle for a fiction book because you can tell them what you are trying to do in one sentence to hook them in. It is powerful marketing for a fiction book just as much as it is for a nonfiction book so that is something to bear in mind.

So next thing to do is build on the promise or benefit of your title. You've got a few more words in your subtitle so you can expand on that by telling them what pain they're going to avoid or what pleasure they're going to gain. You can incorporate the words "you or your" into the book, particularly if this is a how to book that helps somebody with a problem. The words "you and your" make it more personal as if you are speaking to them directly. You get to explain more of what the book is about and again this applies equally to fiction and nonfiction books.

Here is an idea for a nonfiction book. It can be very useful to tell somebody how your book can benefit them, for example you may say it is the "6 Step System for XYZ". So people like the idea that there is a system they can follow and you have broken it down and made it easier for them. For most fiction books you can tell people it is part of a series or trilogy (if it is obviously). If your book is part of a series you are going to make more sales on the front end.

Let's say somebody is looking at 2 books, comparing 2 books, and they like the look of both of them. One is part of a series or a trilogy and one isn't. They are going to buy the one that is part of the series because they want to know that at the end of the book, if they have liked it enough they can carry on reading. So by creating a series, you will get more sales on the front end. So here is the other thing, you get more sales on the back end as well because at the end of your book, you put links to your other books in your series so they can do those impulse purchases where they click the link at the back of your Kindle book and immediately down load the next one.

So you make extra sales on both the front end and back end so make sure you make it clear your book is part of a series. Create mystery, suspense, controversy, and intrigue. Again that applies to both fiction and nonfiction books. Similarly make it sound controversial and interesting. It hooks people in to click on your book and get them a step further towards making a sale. So that is step one, getting a title, a really powerful title and subtitle working together.

Step #2 Create an Eye Popping Book Cover

So step two is getting an eye popping book cover. There are a lot of books on Amazon competing for attention including the books down the side margin that Amazon themselves are advertising. So you are competing against all of that noise. So it is absolutely important that your book stand out and draw the eye. One of the first things you want to achieve with your cover is make sure your title is *easy to read and remember*. Usually upper case is best for your title because it is bigger. Secondly the wording of your title should be in a highly contrasting colour to the background. Remember, people are not seeing the full size version of your cover, they are seeing a little thumbnail on Amazon with 10 or 20 other thumbnails on a page…so make it easy to read.

The subtitle itself does not have to be in upper case but it should still be highly readable. They don't have to necessarily read it as part of the thumbnail. If your title is interesting enough to get them to click on the thumbnail they will go on and read the subtitle. In any case your subtitle should be as readable as you can make it and when you're getting your cover done you want to give very clear instructions to your designer because good design and good marketing must work together.

There are lots and lots of covers on Kindle and Amazon and in regular book stores that look amazing but really don't work very well from a marketing point of view. The design is fantastic, the colours are great, but they miss out on some of the key marketing things like having a highly readable title and so on. So bear in mind that a lot of designers mainly come from a design background only so you need to combine the marketing background in as well for your book cover to be effective.

You need to brief them on these principles when you are getting your book created and as well as having a very good readable title. You want to highlight your book in the sense that it's bright and bold on the page. It doesn't have to be ridiculously garish but it does need to stand out. If it is very neutral in colour, it is not really going to show up very well. So you want bold colours to flash out of the page so when a prospect looks at that arresting image of your cover they can read your title nice and clear in a contrasting colour.

I just want to mention something else as a little side note here. You can use Facebook ads to test a range of covers before you publish your book. All you need to do is simple and doesn't require a lot of money. Just set the Facebook ads up and send people to a squeeze page where you can capture their email. You can do this with different designs until you find the winning design that has the best click through rate. So what does that mean for you and your book?

Imagine translating those clicks into actual sales for your book. By testing on Facebook you can see how many people are clicking on the image for your book. This method is hugely powerful and not expensive. You can spend as little as $50 on Facebook advertising and just devote one day doing it. Nowadays you can also get covers done very, very cheaply. You can use sites like http://www.fiverr.com or http://www.gigbucks.com and get a cover for as little as $5. All you have to do is give them a brief overview of what you want and send them a picture.

Step #3 Get a Great Description Together

Step 3 is to get a great description together. Once you have grabbed their attention with a highly visible cover that pops off the page and an attention grabbing headline, you can then go to the next stage which is the description. It is really important to write a great description that sells your book. Your description is ironically the most important writing you are going to do next to your title and subtitle. Your description is even more important in a sense *than the book itself* because without a great description you are not going to sell the book. So take some time to do this.

Your description should be like a mini sales letter that tells people what the book is about. If it is a *how to* book on how you are going to solve a problem, your book should outline what benefits you are going to give them. If it is a fiction book, you can get them hooked in to wanting to know more about the characters and the plot and give them a really great cliff hanger that will get them real excited about the book.

Here is a top tip about writing your description.

Do not use *Author Central* to add your description. Instead add it *via* your KDP bookshelf. Author Central has a number of formatting issues. If you add your description through Author Central you will only get 2400 characters and you will not be able to go back and edit it through your KDP bookshelf. However, if you add it through KDP bookshelf directly you get 1600 more characters and you have more freedom to edit your description as you please. So please *stay away* from author central and edit your description through the KDP bookshelf.

Here is something else, it is a really good idea to use Amazon HTML code and I will show you how to outsource that in a second. What Amazon HTML code will do is make your books stand out from about 90% of all the other books on Amazon that are just using plain text. Amazon HTML code allows you to do things like make your text bold so that it will stand out more and look more professional. But please consider that HTML coding is included in the 4000 characters you have available...So you want to allow about 600 characters for the HTML code which leaves about 3400 characters for you to work with for your description.

In your description you want to excite and intrigue your prospects. You want to either highlight the pain they will avoid or the benefit they will receive if it is applicable to do so. Use keywords as well because it will help you rank on Amazon search and it is also going to potentially help your book rank on Google as well. Naturally you do not want to stuff keywords in your description. That might have worked 10 years ago but it doesn't work today. Secondly stuffing your description with keywords is going to make your description read badly which will reflect negatively on you as an author and will reduce the number of sales you get.

Similarly don't pad your description. You don't have to use all 3400 characters if you have got a great tight description. Padding it out just reflects badly on you as a writer, especially if there is lots of fluff in there. So don't pad it out and use your keywords sparingly, because it's like a resume for you as a writer. You want to really take your time and do a great description.

How to outsource your description.

You can outsource you description to http://www.fiverr.com and get it done with HTML code. First thing you want to do it just type up a document in Microsoft Word showing how you want the book to look. Always use short paragraphs because it makes it much more readable. By breaking up the text, people will read much more of it. You can use Amazon orange for the title of the book as this again ties in with the website you are selling through. Be sure to use bold, italics, and bullets because many people are trained to see those things as important. So it will get people reading through your description and it gives you a chance to hook them on your book. So make use of all of those things.

I would also recommend that you left justify rather than centre justify. Centre justification looks very unprofessional. So create your document and then go to Fiverr.com and for $5 you can buy a gig where somebody will convert that document into Amazon HTML code. Then all you have to do when you upload your book to KDP and get it available on Kindle is just copy and paste the code you have been sent. So it is super easy and you don't have to know any coding whatsoever. You just have to know what you want it to look like. This method alone will set your book apart from at least 90% of other books on Kindle. So that is how to get a great description done and how to use Amazon HTML.

Step #4 Getting Good Prelaunch Reviews

The next step is getting good prelaunch reviews. It is really important to get some good genuine reviews in place before you really start selling your book. First of all, you are going to have to get it on Kindle and KDP in order to start getting reviews in place. So your book must be published so you can get those reviews in place. Once you have it published you're not going to promote it immediately. You need to leave yourself a couple of week's gap ideally, so you can get all the prelaunch stuff set up before you actually run your launch campaign.

This will give you time to get those reviews in place. Social proof is really important *even if the book is free* because there is still a risk there. The main risk is people's time. People don't want to waste time on a book that turns out to be a flop. Another risk is people don't want to feel stupid even if nobody else is going to know they've downloaded your book. They will feel stupid if they've downloaded something only to find out they don't like it. So it doesn't matter how good your book is they still want some evidence *from other people* before they buy. So you want to get some reviews in place before you launch your book and this will make the difference of thousands of downloads.

Here is why it is important to get those reviews in place.

You can take a book with no reviews at all and run a *free* download campaign and compare it with the exact same book (paid) with half a dozen good reviews and you would get several thousand more downloads with those reviews in place on the *paid version*. Social proof is very important. You also want to make sure that you don't post fake reviews because if you get caught doing that Amazon will take all your reviews down and you could end up getting banned from Amazon with all your content taken down and your account closed. It's just not worth losing your royalties.

So here is what you do. You can ask your fans or followers or people in your industry if you need to send them a review copy. But ideally what you do is set your price to 0.99 cents which is the lowest Amazon will allow you to price your book at and ask them to review the book and actually buy a copy. Now this may be a little bit cheeky, but what it means is when the review is posted it will show as a verified purchase which just gives that review that extra bit of credibility. It tells the perspective customer somebody actually bought the book before they reviewed it. So that is what you do to start getting some reviews in place.

If people who you want to review your book don't have a Kindle, you just make sure they know about the free Kindle app that they can download on pretty much any device. You need about 5-10 reviews to begin with, and obviously the more reviews you get the better. If you have at 5 reviews you are good to go. Get 5 and you're ready to roll.

Step #5 - The KDP free give away.

Now I am going to talk to you about the KDP free give away. This is super easy to set up from the book shelf area of your KDP account which is where you publish your book in the first place. You just have to look under the promotions manager button and you can set it up for whatever days you want. You can do up to 5 days in any 90 day period. You don't have to do all 5 but if it's your first book launch I would recommend using all 5 for the simple fact that you get more and more momentum as the campaign goes on.

What happens next?

So what will happen is when your book is *brand new;* on the first day you will get a few downloads. Fiction books tend to get more than nonfiction books, so as you get those downloads it will start to appear in more places on Amazon amongst the free listings. What will happen on day 2 is you will get more organic downloads as a result. So gradually your book is building momentum. So each successive day, you should get more and more downloads. You will most likely get your maximum number of downloads on day 5. By getting all these downloads we are basically telling Amazon that our book is worthwhile and worth them investing a little bit of their onsite advertising spacing on it.

Just like any other business Amazon is in it to make money; and they aren't going to advertise books that aren't looking like they're going to sell. So by letting Amazon know that your book is worthwhile; Amazon (themselves) will start promoting it for free when the book switches back to *paid* and that is a good thing.

The next thing you're trying to do is tell Amazon where to promote your book. It is no good promoting your book on a page that is not relevant to your target audience. You want your book to be highly targeted. So if you get several thousand downloads, Amazon will cross check all those downloads with other books that people have bought and will start to build up a pattern of where your book would start appearing along with the others. So what you end up with at the end of your free give away is your book showing on highly targeted pages with very similar books all across Amazon. This in turn will *immediately generate a lot of sales* from the moment your book switches back to *paid.*

Many successful sellers on Amazon Kindle have reported seeing their sales go up as much as 1500% when their book switched to *paid*. So this is really powerful stuff and don't worry about giving your book away for free in the beginning. *You're never going to run out of customers!*

If you have a website that goes along with your book, it's also a good idea to have a link to an *opt in page* for your buyers. Again, even if you are a fiction author you want to be building a list because how great would it be when you get your next book out, you can email your list just after you launch it. When it switches back to paid, and you can get a few hundred or even a few thousand people downloading a copy of your book, that is going to rocket it up the best seller charts.

So I highly recommend you get people to opt into your list whether you are fiction or non-fiction writer, if you're a fictional author you might offer them a short story or something like that, so if they like your book and they bought it you can give them a short story and that can be their extra bonus for opting in.

If you want to have proof of your book success, particularly from the point of view of if you are using it as a positioning tool or just for posterity for your own records, you want to pop in quite regularly and take screen shots because Amazon updates their category best seller list basically on an hourly basis so it changes all the time.

If you go to your KDP bookshelf, click on the action button that says "manage promotions" you'll see a box pop up. All you have to do from that point is fill in the 3 fields. You can put in the name of the book, the start date of the promotion, and the finish date. If it's a new book you'll have all 5 days available. So that's it; that is literally how easy it is to set up your free KDP campaign and you don't have to change your price or anything like that. Amazon will change the price for you. They'll automatically switch it to zero and then switch it back to paid at whatever paid price you set at the end of the promotion.

Step #6 Working with the Kindle Book Campaign

Now I am going to go onto step 6. This is what I call the $0.99 cent Kindle book campaign. This is like rocket fuel for your KDP give away.

There are a number of discount Kindle book sites out there. A lot of them are used to just advertise free books but Amazon made some changes to their associates program so some of them now have switched to advertising discounted books. The reason you want to set this up in advance is because a lot of the advertising book slots are getting booked up days and sometimes even weeks in advance. Ideally you want to have several sites that you can advertise on so that you can piggy back off the momentum you're already getting from your free campaign.

So in step 5 I showed you the free giveaway campaign that is going to give you a lot of momentum and generate a lot of organic sales through Amazon anyway. This $0.99 cent book campaign is something you set up for the first couple of days after your book switches back to paid. I'm not suggesting that your book should be priced at $0.99 cents long term, I am only saying you should do this for the first day or two to really make your book into as much of an impulse purchase as you can. Make the barrier to clicking 'buy' on your book as low as you can make it. Amazon will not let you price any lower than $0.99 by the way.

So now what we're going to do is set up our advertising on these high traffic sites that have a lot of social media followers and they send out emails and daily recommendations. You can get in front of literally tens of thousands of avid Kindle book buyers through these. So what this is all doing is really boasting your Amazon rankings so you are getting organic sales from your KDP give away plus you are getting all the people coming in through your advertising as well.

I recommend you spend at least $100 on advertising. If you do it the way I am describing in this book you can make back your advertising costs multiple times within a couple of days. There are lots of sites that do advertise for discounted Kindle books, you want to ideally check http://www.alexa.com, because it allows you to check the rankings of websites. I personally aim for sites that are ranking within the top 250,000 websites worldwide as that way I know they are getting some pretty solid traffic. The higher the traffic; the better. Try to look for anything over 250,000, before actually spending money with those sites. There are some good sites out there and you will get a multiple return on your investment.

So those are the 6 steps to running a Kindle campaign and getting a best seller on Kindle. Once you have done these steps and you've got everything right from the beginning such as great title, great subtitle, you've got the cover that pops, you've got good reviews in place, you've run 2 good promotions, you've run the free promotion, and you've run the paid promotion, you've run the 0.99 cent promotion for a couple of days, switched your book back to whatever it is $3, $5, $8 whatever your price, you will then start reaping the benefits. Because you've set all this up this way you'll keep getting these organic sales for a long time to come without having to go back in and promote the whole thing all over again...so this is really, really powerful stuff!

Chapter 7 - Your Kindle Publishing Opportunity

This brings us to your Kindle publishing opportunity. Now I mentioned this at the beginning of the book, this is your chance if you're not already, to become a published author. It is your chance to become a bestselling author and ideally a number one bestselling author because it is powerful positioning. It's just nice to be able to say that you're a number one best seller. If you want to be an expert you can also sell or promote your business to establish yourself as an expert in your field.

Why publish on Kindle? Well potentially if you put the work in and you get enough titles out and they do well, you have a chance to make a full time income working part time as a writer. You can even outsource the writing as well like I mentioned earlier if you don't want to do it all yourself. It is a good way of building up a big portfolio that gives you a chance to build financial freedom for yourself.

You're getting a long term passive income stream and of course if you've got financial freedom that can generate time as well. You get to live your dream life and of course give yourself the creditability for the rest of your life of being a bestselling author. Once you're a bestselling author, nobody can take that away from you. So that is some reasons why you may want to take this a little bit further and get involved with this Amazon kindle.

Chapter 8 - How to Use Public Domain Products as a Template for Creating Your Books

Instead of simply reselling public domain materials, you can rewrite them instead, giving them a modern twist or tackling them from a different angle, while combining relevant data from your research.

You will see this done successfully by many fiction writers. Seth Grahame-Smith's Pride and Prejudice and Zombies are a good example of this, which is a well-done parody of the beloved Jane Austen classic.

Use PLR Material as another Template for Your Work

If nothing in the old books – which are mostly what the public domain materials are made of – can help you write your own e-book, then how about using PLR instead?

PLR stands for private label rights. When you buy a PLR book, you get intellectual rights to it. Most of the time, it means you can simply change the by-line to your name and sell the book right after. That will not do in most cases, though, since it is likely that you are not its only buyer.

The best way to make use of PLR is to use it as a template and add and modify the content using your research data.

For this chapter, keep in mind that you can use a combination of the methods discussed here. Once you hire a ghost-writer, for instance, you can ask him or her to combine your research with public domain materials or the PLR book you have purchased.

Lastly, the most successful e-books do not just sale copies. They also help you sell products or services in your website. You can do this by inviting your e-book readers from time to time to visit your website and subscribe to your newsletter or join your e-learning group if they wish to know more and similar tips.

Chapter 9 - The Top Websites Where You Can Find Ideas on Which E-books Sell Best

These resources are the best that the Internet has to offer because virtually everything is automated. You only have to know the magic keywords – a.k.a. keywords for your chosen niche – to find out which e-books are selling like hotcakes.

EReaderIQ.com

It has many similar features to Jungle Search and also allows you to search according to review ratings. In any case, if there is something you cannot find at Jungle-Search, this website is a good alternative to check out.

Jungle-Search.com

You can get a lot of in-depth information from this site. What's more, it offers listings for other languages as well, which would be a good thing if you are targeting a bilingual market or you plan on producing your e-book in multiple language formats. You can also search by category or subject (sub-niche), price range, reader age and many other factors.

NovelRank.com

This is a very simple website compared to the above sites, but sometimes simple really works best. In this case, Novel Rank will help you track the sales of any book or e-book sold in Amazon – including yours. What's more, it can also track your sales in Amazon sites for other countries like France and Germany.

Clickbank.com

Many e-book writers prefer to sell their books via Clickbank if they one of their products for affiliate marketing. If you are thinking of using the same approach for your future e-books as well, then you should definitely check out which books made it to Clickbank's bestseller lists.

Amazon.com

Last, but not least don't forget to check out Amazon's own ranking for e-books in your niche. They also offer the best reviews since most Kindle readers are less inclined to visit other websites to post a review when they can do so right away at Amazon.

Keep in mind that each website has its own pros and cons, and they vary depending on what type of information you are looking for. It is best overall then to make use of all of these websites when searching for your e-book's topic. They are all free, anyway!

Also you can go to http://www.amazon.com/gp/bestsellers to find a comprehensive list of products that will give you enough insight as to what people are looking for and how much they are willing to pay for it.

Chapter 10 - More Tips on Promoting Your E-book and getting it Out to The World

Your e-book may not really be the Gospel and able to save souls, but if it can do something that your reader really wants, then strategic promoting will definitely be all you need to kick-start its release in the market. Your e-book will be a runaway success in no time!

When promoting your e-book, you are strongly discouraged from using any paid marketing techniques. Remember the rule about free resources and taking advantage of it? Well, it applies in this case, too!

Forum Marketing

In forum marketing, the trick is to establish your credibility and rapport between you and your readers or you and possible affiliate marketers, fellow writers, and reviewers. It is ideal if you start being active in forums even before your e-book is released. Forums that can help you promote your e-book are the following:

• KindleBoards.com

• EBookGab.com

• MobileRead.com

• Other forums specific to your niche

Blog Marketing

Hopefully you already have one from way back, which means you already have an established presence and readership base online. If not, you might want to start working on getting your blog read first. After that, you can use the blog to market your e-book with the following strategies.

• Share excerpts and sneak peeks of your work

• Post reviews of your work on your blog

• Hold contests to increase awareness of your e-book; require contestants to promote your e-book (e.g. tweeting, liking your

Facebook page et al), with every tweet equivalent to one "entry"

• Use copies of your e-books as their prizes

• Post topics relevant to the subject matter of your e-book then end with an invitation to check your work if they want to know more

Give and Take Marketing

There are, of course, other and more technical words for it like link exchanges but all of them boil down to just one principle, and that is for people to give and take for a mutually beneficial relationship.

• If you perform any of the suggested activities below, it is likely that the other person will do the same for you even without being prompted.

• Post a review on e-books of related subject but those that do not directly compete with yours

• Comment on the other person's blog or be a guest writer on their blog

• Interview another author for your next podcast

• Buy someone else's e-book and they will buy yours

Marketing in Amazon

Here are other ways you can market and which are provided by Amazon itself.

• Amazon Author Page – Use this to have readers get a better feel of your personality and what kind of tone and writing they can expect for your e-book. You can use it to establish your credibility as well.

• Amazon Blog – You get this with your Author Page. Do not copy-paste entries from your other blogs here. Instead, make every entry special and with Amazon users in mind. You can also use this to upload book trailers for your work.

• Tagging – Amazon lets you use a maximum of 15 tags to help improve search results for your e-book.

Chapter 11 - Other Types of Marketing

You are likely to be familiar with how most of the items listed below are used. Take advantage of all of them because – you should know the golden rule by now – they are free resources!

• Social networking – Facebook, LinkedIn, MySpace et al

• Instant Messaging – Yahoo, GTalk, Skype et al

• Chat rooms and chat boards

• Press releases

• Microblogging – Twitter, Tumbler, Plurk et al

• Social bookmarking – Digg, Reddit, et al

• Article Directories – E-zine, Hubpages, EHow, et al

Now that you have reached the very last page of this guide, you are already in possession of all Secrets to Successful Amazon Kindle Business. By now, you are hopefully convinced as well that you can write a bestseller even if you do not have the best writing skills.

Ultimately, content is still king and people will love to read your e-book if you have something worth reading. Good luck on your publishing journey!

Chapter 12 - 59 Places to Submit Your Free KDP Promotion for Your Kindle eBook

1. http://free-kindle-books.deha-solutions.com/promote-your-book/
2. http://www.itswritenow.com/submit-your-book/
3. http://authormarketingclub.com/members/announce-your-free-book
4. http://ereadergirl.com/submit-your-ebook/
5. http://awesomegang.com/submit-your-book

6.   http://www.thatbookplace.com/free-promo-submissions/
7.   http://freekindlefiction.blogspot.com/p/tell-us-about-free-books.html
8.   http://kindlebookpromos.luckycinda.com/?page_id=283
9.   http://slashedreads.com/free-book-page-promotions/
10.   http://freediscountedbooks.com/submit/
11.   http://lovelybookpromotions.com/?page_id=124
12.   http://bookcanyon.com/submitbook/
13.   http://www.mommasaysread.com/author-reviews/author-services/
14.   http://www.iloveebooks.com/for-authors.html
15.
https://docs.google.com/spreadsheet/viewform?formkey=dFEyLTFU
SHREd05KaVItaDdUUkVVNGc6MA#gid=0
16.   http://www.frugal-freebies.com/p/submit-freebie.html
17.   http://www.theereadercafe.com/p/authors.html
18.   http://onehundredfreebooks.com/author-free-kindle-book-submission.html
19.   http://igniteyourbook.com/free-ebook-submission
20.   http://ebookdealofday.com/free-book-feature/
21.   http://ebookdealoftheday.co.uk/free-book-feature/ (UK –
Romance only)
22.   http://www.armadilloebooks.com/submit-free-ebooks/
23.   http://bookfreebies.com/submit-book.php
24.   http://www.pixelofink.com/sfkb
25.   http://ereadernewstoday.com/ent-free-book-submissions/ –
Must have 3 or more reviews and a 4 star rating or above. – Contact
them at least 3 days before your book is scheduled to go free.
26.   http://digitalbooktoday.com/12-top-100-submit-your-free-book-to-be-included-on-this-list/ – The majority of submitted books
that meet the minimum guidelines of 18+ reviews and 4.0+ star
average are listed for up to 3 consecutive free days. For a minimal
fee they will list a limited number of books that have little or no
reviews.

27.   http://www.fkbooksandtips.com/for-authors/free-kindle-promotion/
 - First come, first serve $25 flat fee
28.   http://www.freebookdude.com/2014/03/list-your-free-amazon-kindle-books.html
29.   http://www.totallyfreestuff.com/submit.asp
30.   http://ebookshabit.com/for-authors/
31.   http://bargainebookhunter.com/free-book-notification-form/ - It is recommended that you contact them a week or more in advance of when you have planned your KDP Select free days.
Please include the title, dates your book will be free, and the ASIN or a link to your book on Amazon.
Do not cloak, shorten or include your amazon affiliate code in your life. Such actions will guarantee your book will be ignored!
32.   http://indiebookoftheday.com/authors/free-on-kindle-listing/
33.   http://ebooklister.net/submit.php
34.   http://bookangel.co.uk/submit-your-book/
35.   http://bookdealhunter.com/submit-free-book/ (must be an e-mail subscriber to their blog)
36.   http://bookgoodies.com/submit-your-free-kindle-days/
37.   http://bookpinning.com/?sws=home/submit-book
38.   http://contentmo.com/submit-your-free-ebook-promo
39.   http://freekindlefiction.blogspot.com/p/tell-us-about-free-books.html (fiction only)
40.   http://form.jotformpro.com/form/21078469493969 (for the Kindle Book Review)
41.   http://www.ereaderperks.com/authors/
42.   http://www.ereaderutopia.com/
43.   http://www.freebooks.com/submit/
44.   http://freedigitalreads.com/author-submissions/
45.   http://snickslist.com/books/place-ad/
46.   http://www.kornerkonnection.com/index.html
47.   http://addictedtoebooks.com/free – you must have an account and post it only on the days it is free

48. http://www.worldliterarycafe.com/forum/171 - you must have an account and submit it on only on the days it is free
49. http://www.indie-book-bargains.co.uk/addBook.php
50. http://www.freeebooksdaily.com/p/blog-page_17.html
51. http://ereaderlove.com/contact/
52. http://free-stuff-unlimited.com/contact-us-2/
53. http://www.indieauthornews.com/p/contact-us.html
54. http://www.freebookshub.com/authors/
55. http://dealseekingmom.com/about/contact/
56. http://www.freeebooksblog.com/contact/
57. http://jungledealsandsteals.com/about/contact/
58. http://www.freebookshub.co.uk/authors/
59. http://www.pennypinchinmom.com/contact-me/

Please Note: If you don't want to spend hours on hours submitting your book to free submission sites, you can reduce your submission time to just MINUTES with the following submission tools:

http://bookmarketingtools.com/submission-tool-features.php

This service cost $14.99 but you can also go to http://www.fiverr.com and find someone who can promote your eBook to multiple sites for only $5. When you arrive at this site simply put in "Amazon Kindle Promotion" in the search box.

Here is a sample e-mail you can use for your free eBook promotions. Feel free to adapt it with your own information and use it when you want to send out information.

====================

I wanted to let you know that I'm currently running a special promotion on Amazon Kindle for my newest book (How to Make a Man Fall in Love with you in 90 Days or less) which will be available for free.

Free on Saturday 07/12/14, Sunday 07/13/14 and Monday 07/14/14.
"The Game of Men - How to Make a Man Fall in Love with You in 90 Days or Less!" (ASIN: B00G8L39J4)
http://www.amazon.com/dp/B00G8L39J4

5 reviews with an average 5 star rating

Here is where you can find me online.
Blog: (your blog url)
Facebook: (your Facebook page)
Twitter: (your twitter page URL)

Thanks for letting your readers know about this free book promotion!

~*(Your Name)*

Chapter 13 - ACCESS TO BONUS STEP-BY-STEP VIDEO TUTORIALS

First of all, we'd like to give you a **BIG HEARTY** Thank you for purchasing our book.
We strive to offer you the best service possible and certainly hope that we've been able to give you some kind of ***VALUE for your money's worth!***

If you've learned anything or got at least **1 GOOD IDEA** from our book, we kindly ask that you share that with us and leave some feedback.
Your humble feedback will not only help us to push forward with more helpful products to serve you better, but will also help other lovely customers (such as yourself) to make a purchasing decision as each review will be online for **ALL TO SEE!**

Once Again We Thank You for Your Time with Us and We Wish You **GREAT SUCCESS ON YOUR JOURNEY!**

(Just Click on the Link Below or Copy and Enter It in Your URL, then Copy and Paste the Password in the Box)

http://videoreviewteam.com/amazon-kindle-create-kindle-bestseller-6-simple-steps

Password: amazonkindle6

NOTE: Also If you want ***MORE IN DEPTH ADVANCED TRAINING*** on ***How You Can Earn a 6 Figure Income Making Money on Amazon Kindle*** (There is a Link at the Bottom of the Videos Page) ...**Thank You Once Again!**